이명우 한-영 시선집

Selected Poems of
Myung-Woo Lee
in Korean and English

Selected Poems of
Myung-Woo Lee
in Korean and English
이명우 한-영 시선집

초판인쇄 2022년 4월 5일
초판발행 2022년 4월 11일

지은이_ 이명우
번역_ 구하라
발행인_ 이현자
발행처_ 도서출판 현자

등록_ 제 2-1884호 (1994.12.26)
4F, 50-1, supyo-ro, Jung-gu, Seoul, 04550, Rep. of KOREA
Tel_ (02) 2278-4239
faX_ (02) 2278-4286
E-mail_001hyunja@hanmail.net

값 11,000원

ISBN 978-89-94820-74-3 03810

이명우 한-영 시선집

Selected Poems of Myung-Woo Lee in Korean and English

도서출판 연자

자서

이것저것 여러 가지 제목으로 첫 시집을 출간하고 보니
한 제목이라도 그 언어가 품고 있는 내면세계를 깊고 넓게
살펴보고 조명해보고 규명해보고 싶어졌다
과학은 머리털 하나로 천 갈래 만 갈래로 쪼개는데
문학은 왜 언어 한 개로 천 갈래 만 갈래로 못 쪼개는가
여기에서 언어를 요리하는 시인으로서 자존심이 상했다
내가 해야지 하고 테마 연작시 제목으로 '산골풍경'이란 언어로
시작한 지 올해로 33년이 되지만 아직도 이 한 편의 시가
언제 끝날지 스스로도 모르는 지금 발표한 1100편 중에서
55편을 영역 시선집으로 엮는다.

After publishing my first collections of poetry under random titles, I had an urge to break down, illuminate and scrutiny the depth and width of the inner world that the language within a single title could hold.

Scientists split a single strain of hair into thousands and millions of pieces. So why not a poet split a single language into thousands and millions of pieces.

While thinking about so, my pride as a poet, the chef of language, was shattered.

It has been 33 years since I began writing a single-themed serial poem under the title 'The Scene in the Woods' to rebuild my pride; however, I still do not know when this poem will finish. After all, this book contains English translations of 55 pieces of my 1,100 published poems.

From the author

Table of Contents

- Free Verse -

- Single-themed serial poem -

Free Verse

The first part is free verses included in my first collection of poems.

고찰

고요를 깨뜨리는 풍경소리
천년 리듬으로 쌓이는 뜨락에
여승 같은 모란이 피고
모란 같은 여승이 웃는다

그 따스운 웃음 흘러도
나비는 오지 않고
빛바랜 벽화들만 낮 하늘에 별로 뜨고
봄을 줍는 산새들만 반야경을 외운다

뜨락은 산을 보며 푸르고
산은 하늘을 보며 짙은데
햇빛은 모란을 태우고
모란은 5월을 태운다

An Old Buddhist Temple

The sound of a wind chime breaking the silence,
The rhythm accumulated on the garden for a thousand years.
In the garden, a nun-like peony blossom
And a peony-like nun smile.

Despite the warmth of her smile,
No butterfly comes by.
Only faded murals rise in the daytime sky as stars
And forest birds gleaning the spring chant Prajna-Paramita-Sutra.

While the garden gazing the mountain becomes blue
And the mountain gazing the sky becomes vivid,
The sunlight burns up the peony
And the peony burns up May.

억새꽃

파도치던 여름도
금혼식의 가을도
보고만 있던 억새
겨울 문이 열리고
된서리가 칠 때
하얀 희망으로 피어나는 꽃
파란 하늘을 펴 놓고
자화상을 그리고 있나 보다

낮이면 구름을 불러 바둑을 두고
밤이면 생각을 풀어 비밀을 줍는

겨울을 지고 가는 꽃
겨울을 타고 가는 꽃

Silvergrass

Silvergrass only stared at
The overwhelming waves in the summer
And the Golden Wedding in the fall.
When the door to the winter opened
And hit by a heavy frost,
The flower blossomed as a white hope,
Spreading out the blue sky,
Drawing a self-portrait.

Playing go with the clouds in the day,
Gleaning secrets untying the mind in the night,

The flower carrying the winter,
And the flower riding the winter.

생각

휘파람 불면서 흔들리는 노송은
때리는 눈으로 옷을 기워 입고
산 이마를 누르는 구름을 보고 있다

살얼음 부서지는 강에
떠내려 오는 산 너머 소식
이 몸에 불을 질러
어머님 차가운 방에 군불로 타고 싶다

시린 마음 기도로 녹여
산딸기로 맺어서
아침상 한 접시에 오르고 싶다

In my mind

The old pine tree blowing in the wind, whistling,
Mending clothes with striking snow,
Is glancing at the cloud pressing down the mountain forehead.

Through the river with thin ice breaking,
A tiding from over the mountain floated down.
I yearn to set myself on fire
To burn as fuel to heat the mother's cold room.

To melt my cold heart with prayer
And bear a wild berry
To be served on a plate for her breakfast.

하늘을 내 앞으로 등기해 놓고

눈물 세계 그 위에
웃음 세계 그 위에
시의 세계 여기에 와 살자

8각 도장을 새겨라

하늘을 내 앞으로 등기해 놓거든
아내여 비를 들고 별을 쓸어 모아라
굵은 별은 골라서 목걸이를 만들고
잔별은 씻어서 밥을 짓자

Once I register the heaven in my name

In the world of tears,
In the world of laughter,
In the world of poetry, let us come and live here.

Engrave an octagon signet.

Once I register the heaven in my name,
Dear wife, take the broomstick and sweep to gather the stars.
Let us make a necklace with big stars
And cook rice with tiny stars.

변심

와서는 말했어요
그리운 추억이었노라고
말하고는 울었어요
다시 갈순 없노라고
울다가 지쳐버린 아픈 소망은
용서를 비는 뜻은 더욱 아녀요
몹쓸 것이기에 단념하셨겠지만
어쩌다 생각이 나실 때에는
진종일 이를 갈며 욕해주세요
그래도 아직 메스꺼우면
변심의 얇은 가슴 더러운 이 몸을
갈가리 찢기도록 곤장을 쳐서
언약하던 강변 숲에 버려주세요

밝은 달이 돋아 올라 남 보기 전에
검은 구름 내리 덮어 비 오기 전에

Betrayal

You came and spoke to me
That you still miss those days.
Spoke and wept,
Because you cannot go back.
The painful hope that got tired of crying
Does not mean I am begging for forgiveness.
You must have given up on me for my cruelty.
When you think of me sometimes,
Curse me all day, gnashing your teeth.
If you are still disgusted,
Flog my thin heart of betrayal and unclean body,
Until it is ripped apart
And abandon in the woods by the river where we made a vow.

Before a bright moon rises so that others can see,
Before black clouds cover up the sky and pour down rain.

망향

평화로운 봄의 태양이
꽃잎에서 시름없이 존다

강남에서 굴러오는 오현금에
한 쌍의 나비
음률 따라 오르내리며 춤추고
그 나래에 부리어 봄바람이 인다

봄바람에 쫓겨 저 구름 가는 하늘
그 아래 앉은 동네
심고 온 산작약이 이초 따라 크는 소리
오늘따라
고향 리듬에 빠진 마음은
점점 깊숙이 가라앉는다

Homesickness

A peaceful spring sun
Drowses dispirited on a flower petal.

A pair of butterflies
Dance up and down to the melody
Of Pentachord playing from Gangnam
And their wings trigger the spring breeze.

A cloud chased by the spring breeze in the sky.
Under the sky sits a small village.
The sound of woodland peony growing with peculiar flowers and plants.
Today,
My heart immersed in the rhythm of the hometown
Sinks deeper and deeper.

병신춤 시대

칼을 들이대도 웃는 아기는
평화만 보이기 때문일까요
불속으로 뛰어드는 나비는
꽃만 보이기 때문일까요
속이고 빼앗고 가로채는 건
이기주의만 보이기 때문일까요

반만년 우리 문화는
단칼에 목이 잘리고
수입문화로 꾸며놓은 무대 위에서
이 시대가 마약을 먹고
꼬부랑 언어로 대사를 외며
정신병자인 줄도 모르고
우리 모두 병신춤을 추는 중입니다

The Age of Byeongsin Dance

Does a baby with a knife on the throat smile
Because the baby only could see peace?
Does a butterfly fly into a fire
Because the butterfly only could see flowers?
Do people deceive, steal, and rob
Because they only could see egotism?

Our five millennia-old culture
Beheaded with a single swing.
On the stage adorned with foreign culture,
This drugged era,
Utters lines with twisted tongue,
Unaware of its insanity,
All dance the Byeongsin Chum[1)]

1) Byeongsin Chum: A Korean folk dance that was performed by the lower class peasants to satirize the Korean nobility (Yangban) by depicting them as the handicapped, for example, paraplegics, midgets, hunchbacks, the deaf, the blind and the lepers. (Byeongsin chum, Wikipedia, 2021)

생각

휘파람 불면서 흔들리는 노송은
때리는 눈으로 옷을 기워 입고
산 이마를 누르는 구름을 보고 있다

살얼음 부서지는 강에
떠내려 오는 산 너머 소식
이 몸에 불을 질러
어머님 차가운 방에 군불로 타고 싶다

시린 마음 기도로 녹여
산딸기로 맺어서
아침상 한 접시에 오르고 싶다

In my mind

The old pine tree blowing in the wind, whistling,
Mending clothes with striking snow,
Is glancing at the cloud pressing down the mountain forehead.

Through the river with thin ice breaking,
A tiding from over the mountain floated down.
I yearn to set myself on fire
To burn as fuel to heat the mother's cold room.

To melt my cold heart with prayer
And bear a wild berry
To be served on a plate for her breakfast.

Single-themed serial poem

The second part is a selection from
my serial-themed poem titled
'The Scene in the Woods: 1~1,100'.

산골풍경: 1

거짓말 같았다
소나기가 왔다는 소리가

안개도 이삿짐을 지고
시지프스의 가쁜 숨결로 산을 넘고
등목하고 나온 햇살
아직
젖어 있는 버드나무 머리칼을 빗질 하고 있다

나리꽃을 터뜨린 나비 한쌍이
하늘로 오르며 꿈을 실어 나르고
불어나는 도랑물이 빚어내는 풍금소리
산 너머 가는 구름
그늘로 춤을 춘다

마음 팔매 원을 그린 먼 하늘에
낮달로 뜬 술잔에 고여 있는 유년을
바라보다 바라보다 장승이 된다

The Scene in the Woods: 1

The news that rain shower came by
Sounded like a lie.

Fog carrying its swag,
Crossed a mountain gasping like Sisyphus.
Sunshine came out after deungmok[2)]
Is yet
Combing the hair of a wet willow tree.

A pair of butterflies which bloomed lilies
Carry up dreams toward the sky,
And clouds crossing a mountain
Dance with their shadows
To the sound of the reed organ formed by an overflowing stream.

I look again and again becoming a Jangseung[3)]
At youth lingering in the whiskey glass as the daytime moon
In the faraway sky, where the ripple of my heart is drawn.

2) Deungmok: An act of splashing water onto the back of another person bending downward in a reversed v-shape. (Deungmok, Korean-English Learners' Dictionary, 2021)

3) Jangseung: Village guardian; A stone or wooden post with a human face engraved on it that is erected at the entrance of a village or a roadside. In a literary context, it indicates extreme nostalgia that became chronic. (Jangseung, Korean-English Learners' Dictionary, 2021)

산골풍경: 105

아내야 나와 봐
무지개에다 그네를 매어 놨어

발 포개고 손 맞잡아
우리
쌍그네 타자
내가 밀면 그대는
별 하나 따서 먹고
그대가 밀면 나는
꿈 한 송이 따서 줄게

아내야 우리 이렇게
구만 년만 살자

The Scene in the Woods: 105

My dear wife, come and see,
I hung a swing on the rainbow for you.

Step on my feet and hold my hands.
Let us
Ride the swing together.
When I push, you
Pick a star to eat.
When you push, I
Will pick a flower of a dream for you.

My dear wife, let us live like this
Just for ninety thousand years.

산골풍경: 114

아버님이 읊으시던
한시 한 편은
풍경소리 위에 앉아
하늘 한 바퀴를 돌아
고향 산하에
흰 눈으로 내립니다

The Scene in the Woods: 114

A piece of Chinese poetry
That my father used to recite
Sat on the sound of a wind chime,
Flew around the sky,
And came down as white snow
On the mountain of my hometown.

산골풍경: 121

내 눈동자에 지어놓은
초가삼간 집 한 채를
전세 내어 살고 있는
여인이 있습니다

추우면 그 여인은
노래하는 봄 햇살로 내리고
더우면 그 여인은
겨울바람으로 춤을 춥니다

이제 보니 나도
그 여인의 눈동자에 초가집을 지어놓고
낮이면 그 여인의 눈동자에서 놀고
밤이면 그 여인의 꿈속에서 삽니다

The Scene in the Woods: 121

In the apple of my eyes,
I built a three-room thatched cottage.
And there lives a woman
Who rented the place.

When it is cold, the woman
Rays down as a singing spring sunlight.
When it is hot, the woman
Dances as a winter wind.

Now I see,
I, too, built a thatched cottage in the apple of her eyes.
In the day, I frolic in the apple of her eyes
And in the evening, I live in her dreams.

산골풍경: 123

해맑은 달빛이
도랑물과 몸을 섞어
결혼식을 치르는 밤

바닷속 고기들이
기별을 듣고
축의금을 물고와
파문따라 춤을 추고
산새들도 잠을 설치고
꽃다발을 들고와
덤불 사이에서 축가를 부르는 밤

나는 불청객으로
자연의 결혼식을
훔쳐보고 있다

The Scene in the Woods: 123

The night of the wedding,
When the sunny moonlight
Makes love to the stream of water.

The night when fish in the ocean
That heard the news
Carries the wedding gift
Dancing to the ripple,
And birds in the woods staying up all night
Bring bouquets
Singing for the wedding in the bushes.

I, the unwelcomed guest,
Am peeping
At the wedding of nature.

산골풍경: 134

보름달 8번지에
모래성을 쌓아 놓고
산나리로 피어서
웃고 있는 저 여인은

추억의 강가에
그리움을 심어 놓고
보름달로 이사 가서
혼자 사는 그 여인

The Scene in the Woods: 134

That smiling woman
Who built a sandcastle
On 8 Full Moon Street
And bloomed as a gold-rayed lily

Is the woman who lives alone
On the full moon,
After planting her yearning
By the river of remembrance.

산골풍경: 146

쓰레기통에 버려진
몽당연필이
나를 보며 웃습니다

덕지덕지 묻은
내 손때를
훈장처럼 둘르고
절대 순종으로
나를 섬기다가
나에게 버림을 받고도
나를 보고 웃고 있는
일편단심의 몽당연필

나는 마지막 날
세상이 나를 버렸을 때
세상을 보며 웃을 수 있을까
몽당연필이 가르쳐 준
일편단심의 교훈을
가슴에 안고 눈감고 있다

The Scene in the Woods: 146

From the trash can,
An abandoned stubby pencil
Smiles at me.

With dirty stains
Of my finger marks
Berobed like a medal,
It served me
With absolute obedience.
Though abandoned,
The loyal stubby pencil
Smiles at me.

On my last day,
When the world abandons me,
Will I be able to smile at the world?
The lesson taught by the stubby pencil,
The lesson of loyalty,
I dearly hold in my arms, eyes closed.

산골풍경: 187

산새가 날아와
그러는데
인생은 불고 가는
바람이 아니라
꿈꾸는 열일곱 살로
움트는 봄이래요

The Scene in the Woods: 187

Bird in the woods flew by
And told me
That life is not
A brushing wind
But a springtime
Sprouting like a dreaming 17-year-old.

산골풍경: 200

내가 날마다 불을 질러서
까맣게 타버린 어머니의 마음은
하얀 재가 되어 훨훨 날아다니시더니
이 산 능선에 내려와
백도라지 꽃으로 피어 있네요

어머니요 불렀더니
대답 대신에
하얀 웃음만 지으시네요

갑니다 인사하니
아무 말 없이
향 내음을 한아름 안겨주네요

조각조각 심장을 쪼개 먹여 주시던
야삼경에 일어나 칠성님께 소원 빌던
어머니는 이 산에 와 새색시가 되었습니다

The Scene in the Woods: 200

My mother's heart burned black
Because I set fire to it every day.
Her heart became white ash gliding through the air,
Came down to this mountain ridge,
And bloomed into balloon flowers.

Mother! I called out.
Instead of an answer,
Smiled a white smile.

I am leaving, I greeted.
Without words,
Handed me an armful of fragrance.

The one who fed us her heart piece by piece,
And prayed to the Great Bear every midnight,
Mother came to this mountainside and became a newlywed.

산골풍경: 232

아내야 우리
추억의 호미를 들고
세월속에 묻어 둔
청춘을 캐러 가자

세월을 파 헤치고
또 파헤쳐서
그 속에 묻혀 있는
열여덟 살 그대를 찾고
열아홉 살 나도 찾아
세월 없는 세계로
이사 가서 살자

The Scene in the Woods: 232

Dear wife, let us
Pick up the hoe of old memories,
Dig out our youth
Buried in time.

Dig up the time
Again and again
To find the buried
18-year-old you
And 19-year-old me,
Move into the world
Without time and live happily ever after.

산골풍경: 236

초승달이 혼자서 마실 가다가
달려드는 먹구름에 깜짝 놀라
포르르 날아와 내 가슴에 숨어서
무서워요 무서워요 떨고 있다

그래 그래 무서운 세상
사람 세계에도 무서움이 있지
가만히 쳐다보며 내 이야기 듣다가
내 품에서 새록새록 잠든 초승달

The Scene in the Woods: 236

The new moon went on a trip by herself,
Appalled by swarming black clouds,
Flew into my arms, quivering,
Saying, "I am scared, I am scared," trembling.

"There, there! It's a dangerous world.
In the world of men, there also is fear."
Glancing and listening to my words,
The new moon laid fast asleep in my arms.

산골풍경: 281

아들아
강해서 부서지는
이빨처럼 살지 말고
부드러워 평생 가는
혀처럼 살그래이

아들아
칼 끝으로 매서운
겨울바람처럼 살지 말고
꿈을 꾸는 따뜻한
봄바람처럼 살그래이

아들아
너 혼자만 생각하는
짐승처럼 살지 말고
세상을 품어 주는
천사처럼 살그래이

아들아 이런 가훈이 우리집의 핏줄이데이
이 핏줄을 너도 물려주거래이

The Scene in the Woods: 281

My son,
Do not live like teeth
That shatters by its hardness.
Live like a tongue
That lasts a lifetime by its softness.

My son,
Do not live like a winter wind
That is sharp as a sword.
Live like a spring breeze,
Dreaming and warm.

My son,
Do not take care only of yourself
Like a beast,
But live like an angel
Who embraces the world.

My son,
This family motto
Runs in the blood of our family.
Pass down this blood
To your descendants.

산골풍경: 325

아름다운 착각은
아름다운 행운입니다
멋진 시인으로 착각하며
살아가고 있는 나
가슴에 타는 불길도
멋진 시 한 편으로 보입니다

아름다운 공상은
아름다운 꽃입니다
하늘을 내 앞으로
등기해 놓고 보니
천하 제일 부자도
비렁뱅이로 보입니다

아름다운 실패는
아름다운 성공입니다
자빠지고 엎어지면서도
꿈을 꾸며 일어나 보니
승리의 행복이
파도치고 있습니다

The Scene in the Woods: 325

Beautiful illusion
Is a beautiful fortune.
My illusion
Of being a great poet,
Lead me to set the fire burning inside my heart
As a great piece of poetry.

Beautiful daydream
Is a beautiful flower.
Once I register
The heaven in my name,
Even the richest man in the world
Looks like a beggar in my eyes.

Beautiful failure
Is a beautiful success.
Hoping and standing on two feet
While tumbling and falling,
Pleasure of happiness
Rushed like the wave.

산골풍경: 401

잠든 아내를 들여다보다가
가슴을 톡톡 두드렸더니
속이 텅텅 비어 있는 소리
배를 톡톡 두드려 봐도
간도 없고 쓸개도 없고 심장도 없는
속이 텅텅 비어 있는 소리

이제야 내 눈에 눈물 한 방울 나온다
맨 처음 간을 꺼내 나를 먹여 주다가
큰 놈이 생겨서는 쓸개를 꺼내 먹여 주고
작은 놈이 생겨서는 심장을 꺼내 먹여 주어
이제는 줄 것이 없는 속이 텅빈 빈껍데기 아내
선풍기를 틀었더니
잠이든 채로 붕붕 풍선처럼 떠다닌다

The Scene in the Woods: 401

Gazing at my sleeping wife,
I tapped her bosom.
It made an empty sound.
I tapped her belly.
It made an empty sound,
As if she has no liver, no gall bladder, and no heart.

Eventually, a drop of tear came out.
First, she fed me her liver,
Then she fed our firstborn her gall bladder,
Then she fed our youngest her heart.
Now my wife became an empty shell with no organs to feed.
When I put on a fan,
When I put on a fan, she floated around like a balloon, sleeping.

산골풍경: 410

내 하얀 그리움
천만리 저 아래 강으로 흐르고

내 파란 아픔
천만리 저 봉우리로 솟아 있네

다 못한 이야기는
무지개 선을 따라 이슬로 맺혀 있고

다 끝난 사연은
저 사막 속에 봉분 없이 묻혀 있네

The Scene in the Woods: 410

My white yearning
Flows down 4 million kilometers as a river.

My blue pain
Is lifted above 4 million kilometers as a mountain peak.

Unfinished conversations
Form dew drops along the rainbow.

Completed stories
Are buried in the desert without a gravestone.

산골풍경: 440

기침 한 번으로
천하를 떨게 하는 동물이 있습니다

어느 날 그 동물은
싸움에서 패배하여
천하를 빼앗기고도
울부짖지 못하고 있습니다

아내도 빼앗기고
영토도 빼앗긴 저 수사자
어쩜 이 세상 모든
수컷들의 운명입니다

The Scene in the Woods: 440

There is an animal that makes the world shiver
With a cough.

One day the animal has
Lost its fight,
Lost its realm,
And lost its voice.

The male lion
Who has lost his wife
And lost its domain!
Maybe it is the fate
Of all males on this Earth.

산골풍경: 452

고운 꿈을 접어 날린
추억의 하늘에
그리움이 나비 되어
날아오는 이 가을날
천연색 사연들은
흰 구름 되어
피고 지는 꽃놀이를 하고 있다
그 사이로 흘러가는
아득한 생애의 강 끝에서
은은하게 들려오는 세월의 종소리를
나 혼자서 가만히 새겨듣고 있다

The Scene in the Woods: 452

On this autumn day,
Yearning transformed into a butterfly
Flies back to me under the sky of memories
Where I flew an origami of my tender dream.
Stories in technicolor
Becomes a white cloud,
Playing bloom and fall of flowers.
From the distant end of the river of life
Flowing between cloud,
I am listening to the gentle chime of time
Alone in stillness.

산골풍경: 520

글을 몰라 다리를 걷고
아버지의 회초리로
종아리를 맞을 때는
한순간만 아팠어요

살 줄을 몰라 생활의 터전에서
운명의 회초리로
인생의 종아리를 두들겨 맞고는
아직도 아파라
뼛속까지 아파라

The Scene in the Woods: 520

When I could not read,
I rolled up my trousers
And father caned my calves.
However, the pain was brief.

When I did not live right
On the stage of life,
The cane of fate beat my calves of life.
It still hurts,
Painful to the bones.

산골풍경: 574

살랑이는 봄바람아
내 마음을 흔들지 마라
그렇잖아도 나는 지금
앞뒤도 보지 않고 줄행랑칠까 하고 있다

사무치는 사연아
잠자는 추억을 깨우지 마라
가슴 부풀던 그날들이
이제는 송곳이 되어 자신을 찌를 것만 같다

피우지 못한 운명아
내 얼굴 앞에서
맴돌지 마라
누군가가 건드리면
고였던 눈물이 펑펑 쏟아질 것만 같다

The Scene in the Woods: 574

Oh, swaying spring breeze
Do not shake my heart.
Though you do not, right now
I want to run away blind.

Oh, smoldering stories,
Do not awaken my sleeping memories.
The days of buoyed heart
Might pierce me like an awl.

Oh, the fate that never bloomed,
Do not linger
In front of my face.
If anyone touches me,
I might shed a tear piled up for a lifetime.

산골풍경: 600

내 인생은 가랑비였나 봐
메마른 가슴 한번 촉촉이 적시지 못했어요

내 운명은 실바람이었나 봐
내 몸 한번 저 하늘로 띄우지 못했어요

내 사랑은 무정란이었나 봐
보듬어 품었어도 꽃망울이 안 보여요

이렇듯 내 인생은
바람 속을 떠도는 노래입니다

The Scene in the Woods: 600

My life maybe was a sprinkle of rain.
It never has wholly wet my dry heart.

My life maybe was a wisp of wind.
It has never floated my body above the sky.

My love maybe was an infertile egg.
There is no flower bud even after prolonged incubation.

As such, my life
Is a song wandering in the wind.

산골풍경: 601

바다보다 넓고 하늘보다 높은
부모님의 은혜를 이제야 알았습니다
부모님의 자식이 된 것이
천천만만 행운임을 이제야 알았습니다
부모님이 지렁이였다면
나는 지금
캄캄한 땅속에서 굴을 파고 있을 겁니다
부모님이 뱀이었다면
나는 지금
풀 속이나 시궁창 속을 기어가고 있을 겁니다
부모님의 전갈이었다면
나는 지금
물 한 방울 없는 뜨거운 사막을
헤매고 있을 겁니다
이렇듯 부모님은 나를 사람으로 세상에 보내 주셨기에
천사 중에 천사로 살고 있습니다
이제야 부모님이
하느님 중에 하느님임을 알았습니다

The Scene in the Woods: 601

Wider than the ocean, higher than the sky.
Now I realize the grace of my parents.
Being your son
Was thousands and millions of blessings.
If you were worms,
I might be
Digging a hole in the dark ground.
If you were snakes,
I might be
Creeping on grass or a sewer.
If you were scorpions,
I might be
In the desert without a drop of water,
Wandering.
Since you sent me to this world as a human,
I am living like an angel of angels.
Now I know
You are gods of gods.

산골풍경: 656

나는 늦바람이 났습니다
어제는 보름달 여인의 젖을 더듬었고
오늘은 샛별 여인의 저고리를 벗겼고
내일은 하느님의 셋째 딸과
극장표를 예약해 놓았습니다

나도 모르게 내 입이 귀에 걸렸나 봐요
나도 모르게 내가 히죽이죽 웃었나 봐요

손자놈 좀 보아요
할아버지 치매 걸리셨나요
아들놈 좀 보셔요
쯧쯧, 아직은 그러실 나이가 아닌데
아내 좀 보셔요
예야 정신병원 어디 있나 찾아 보아라
그런데 나 좀 보셔요
바람피운 이야기는 못하고 그냥 껄껄껄

The Scene in the Woods: 656

I am an old man having an affair.
Yesterday I groped the bosoms of lady full moon.
Today I stripped the corset of Venus.
Tomorrow, I booked tickets
To watch a movie with god's third daughter.

Despite myself, I am smiling.
Despite myself, I am giggling.

Hear my grandson saying,
"Are you demented?"
Hear my son saying,
"Tsk tsk, you are too young to get demented."
Hear my wife saying,
"Hey, son, find him a loony bin."
But look at me
Laughing aloud because I cannot say a word about the affair.

산골풍경: 659

야생화 향기를 바구니에 따 담아와
물레에 감아 실로 뽑는다
뽑아낸 하얀 실타래
뜨개질을 할까
자수를 놓을까
매듭을 엮을까
무슨 작품을 빚어야 하나
꿈만 꾸고 있습니다

The Scene in the Woods: 659

I picked up the scents of the wildflowers,
Spun the wheel to make yarn,
And spooled white thread.
Shall I knit with it?
Shall I embroider with it?
Shall I knot with it?
What shall I make?
Just dreaming about it

산골풍경: 677

저녁노을 오려서
치마를 접고
밤안개를 오려서
저고리를 접어
딸 아이 생일날 선물했더니
아 이런
볼 줄도 모르고
입을 줄도 모르고

The Scene in the Woods: 677

I cut out a sunset,
And fold it into a skirt.
Then cut out a night fog,
And fold it into a jeogori[4].

Gave them to my daughter as her birthday present.
Oh,
What a poor sense of fashion,
She doesn't even know how to wear them!

4) Jeogori: A traditional Korean upper garment. (Jeogori, Korean-English Learners' Dictionary, 2021)

산골풍경: 710

독신으로 사는 것은 이런 거야
저 하늘을 보아
비도 오고 바람 불고
해도 뜨고 달도 뜨지

결혼해서 사는 것은 이런 거야
저 하늘을 보아
비도 오고 바람 불고
해도 뜨고 달도 뜨지

인생은 이런 거야
저 하늘을 보아
비도 오고 바람 불고
해도 뜨고 달도 뜨지

The Scene in the Woods: 710

If you are single,
When you look in the sky,
Rain comes, and the wind blows,
The sun rises, then the moon rises.

If you are married,
When you look in the sky,
Rain comes, and the wind blows,
The sun rises, then the moon rises.

If you are alive,
When you look in the sky,
Rain comes, and the wind blows,
The sun rises, then the moon rises.

산골풍경: 760

소쩍새 울음 소리가
밤바람을 타고 파도 치는 밤
먼먼 그리움이
파도에 밀려와
저 하늘 소복소복
별로 총총 박히는 밤
내 마음의 문구멍에는
세상이 들락날락인다

The Scene in the Woods: 760

When the sound of a scops owl
Surges through the night breeze,
A distant longing
Rushes towards me like waves,
And nestles in the sky like stars
As if stepping on the snow.
Through the keyhole of my heart,
The universe goes in and out.

산골풍경: 763

날아가는 구름 위에 지어놓은
우리 집에 앉아 내려다봅니다
우리 집은 가만 있는데
우리 집 아래엔
산이 지나가고
강이 지나가고
바다가 지나가고 있습니다
쳐다보니
별도 지나가고
달도 지나가고 있습니다
이렇듯 우리 집은
내려다봐도
쳐다봐도
천연색 영화가 상영되고 있습니다

The Scene in the Woods: 763

I sat down and looked down from my house
That I built on a flying cloud.
My house never moved.
But under my house,
The mountain passes by,
The river passes by,
And the ocean passes by.
When I look more closely,
The stars pass by
And the moon passes by.
When I look down
Or look closely
From my house,
A technicolor movie is playing.

산골풍경: 770

열심히 열심히 살다 보면
그 강 건너에
즐겁게 즐겁게 사는
세상이 보입니다

즐겁게 즐겁게 살다 보면
그 강 건너에
미쳐서 미쳐서 사는
세상이 보입니다

미쳐서 미쳐서 살다 보면
그 강 건너에
어느새 다 이루어져
있음이 보입니다

The Scene in the Woods: 770

If you live diligently,
You can see
The world of happiness
Across the river.

If you live happily,
You can see
The world of craziness
Across the river.

If you live like crazy,
You can see
Everything accomplished
Across the river.

산골풍경: 799

손자 녀석 눈동자를
가만히 보았더니
보름달 아홉 개가 뛰어놀고 있습니다

아내의 눈동자를
가만히 보았더니
인연 아홉 개가 뛰어놀고 있습니다

내 눈동자를
가만히 보았더니
운명 아홉 개가 뛰어놀고 있습니다

The Scene in the Woods: 799

At the apple of my grandson's eyes,
I stared.
There, nine full moons were playing around.

At the apple of my wife's eyes,
I stared.
There, nine nidanas were playing around.

At the apple of my eyes,
I stared.
There, nine fates were playing around.

산골풍경: 828

뒷산에 혼자 사는
신선의 초대를 받고
아침 먹으로 가 보았습니다

별쌀로 지은 별밥에
저녁노을 뜯어서 쌈으로 올리고
구름 속 잎 김치에
무지개 한토막 구워 놓고
달빛으로 끓인 국

이 산골에 살다 보니
나도 신선이 되어 가나봐요
이런 음식을 다 먹어 보고요

The Scene in the Woods: 828

From the mountain at the back of the house,
A hermit living alone sent an invitation
To join for breakfast.

On star-made star-shaped rice,
He tore out the sunset and put it as a wrap for rice,
Made leaf kimchi with clouds,
Baked a piece of rainbow,
And boiled soup of moonlight.

Living in the mountains
Made me become a hermit, too.
I am having all these foods.

산골풍경: 840

광한루를 휘어 감고 춤추는 밤바람은
버드나무로 가락을 퉁기며 월궁가를 부르고

연못가를 거닐며 소풍 나온 저 달은
파문으로 그림을 그리며 시를 쓰고 있네

하늘을 버리고 여기에 와 살리라
뛰어내린 별들이 잉어가 되어 지느러미를 흔들고

이곳을 지키리라 일만이천 순절한 넋이
닭이 되어 남원을 품고 볏을 세우고 있네

The Scene in the Woods: 840

The night breeze that winds and dances around the Gwanghallu
Sings the song of the moon while plucking strings of willows.

The moon walks by the pond for a picnic
Paints pictures and writes poems with ripples.

The starts that abandoned the sky and jumped down
Turned into carps and waved their fins.

Twelve thousand martyred souls that pledged to protect this place
Became roosters and lifted their combs, embracing Namwon.

산골풍경: 930

산할아버지
산할아버지
우째서 우리나라 국회의원
300명 다 팔아도
스웨덴 국회의원 한 명을 몬 산다능교
허허, 이 사람아
우리나라 국회의원은
국민 머리 꼭대기로 올라가
호령하며 살지만
스웨덴 국회의원은
국민 발바닥 밑으로 내려가
국민을 섬기며 산다잖는가
우리나라 국회의원
차도 보고 비서들도 보고 월급 봉투 보게나
저들 맘대로 하잖는가
스웨덴 국회의원은
자전거로 출퇴근 비서팀도 없고 사무실도 없고
월급도 날품팔이와 똑같이
일당제로 받는다잖는가

퇴직하면 연금도 없다 잖는가
그런데
하느님도 부러워할
하루만 출근해도
평생 연금을 받는 희한한 사람들
이 나라엔
저런 스웨덴 국회의원 같은 사람
백년이면 하나 나올까
천년이면 하나 나올까

The Scene in the Woods: 930

Mountain spirit,
Mountain spirit,
Why can't we sell members of the National Assembly,
All 300 of them,
And buy a single member of the Swedish parliament?
Huh huh, man,
Our country's lawmakers
Climb on the top of the people's heads
And give commands.
The Swedish Parliamentarian
Low down under the people's feet
And live to serve them.
Look at our lawmakers;
Their cars, secretaries, and pay envelopes.
They do everything as they please.
The Swedish Parliamentarian
Commute on bicycles, has no team of secretaries nor offices,
And paid like a day laborer,
In daily wage.

There is no pension after retirement.
However,
Even god will envy these strange people
Whose single day of work
Pays for their lifelong pension.
On this land,
Will Swedish-minded lawmakers ever exist?
Maybe one in a century?
Or one in a millennium?

산골풍경: 936

이 산골 원두막에
올라와 보면
달나라 초등학교가
보입니다
다시 가만 귀를 귀울이면
그 학교 풍금 소리가 들립니다
풍금 소리를 듣습니다
아 깜짝
우리노래 아리랑이 흘러나와요
또 깜짝
지구 대표곡으로 수입한 아리랑 노래
달나라에서도 대표곡으로 불린대요

The Scene in the Woods: 936

When I go up
To the summerhouse in the woods,
I see
The Lunarian Elementary School.
When I listen closely,
I hear reed organs from the school.
I listen to the reed organs playing.
Oh, what a surprise.
Our song "Arirang"[5)] is playing.
Again, what a surprise.
The Earth exported its anthem "Arirang" to the moon.
It is now the anthem of the moon, too.

5) Arirang: The most famous Korean folk song, containing "Arirang" in its refrain, whose lyrics, melody, etc., vary in different regions. (Arirang, Korean-English Learners' Dictionary, 2021)

산골풍경 : 945

꽃이 피네요
봄이 왔나 봐요
가슴이 떨리네요
청춘이 왔나 봐요
다리가 떨리네요
노년이 왔나 봐요

꽃 피는 봄만
가슴 떨리는 청춘만
있게 해 달라고
하느님께
일곱 번이나
등기 편지를 부쳤는데도
감감 무소식이네요

The Scene in the Woods: 945

Flowers are blooming.
It must be spring coming.
My heart is trembling.
It must be youth coming.
My legs are shaking.
It must be my last day coming.

Let me live
Only in the blooming spring
As a heart-pounding youth.
For seven times,
I wrote registered letters,
Begging.
But there is no reply.

산골풍경: 964

아내야
앞산에 핀
무지개를 걷어 왔어
무얼 만들까

색동옷을 접어요
꽃 이불도 좋고요

아니야, 2인용 비행기 접어 타고
우리 우주로 소풍가자

The Scene in the Woods: 964

Darling,
I've picked the rainbows
From the front hills.
What shall we make?

Let's make a saekdong-ot[6].
A flower blanket sounds good, too.

No, let's make a two-seater plane,
And take a trip to outer space.

6) Saekdong-ot: Rainbow-striped garment; Clothes made by using lots of different colors. It was worn by children aged 5-7 during festive season of South Korea. (Saekdong-ot, Korean-English Learners' Dictionary, 2021)

산골풍경: 965

아내 생일
간밤에 따온
샛별을 왼 가슴에 달아주고
서툰 솜씨로 밥을 짓는다
아내가 좋아하는
찔레꽃 향기로 밥을 짓고
비익조 알탕에
이슬 한 접시 볶아 놓고
달나라에서 따온
딸기도 얹어 놓고
저승에서 캐온
삼지구엽초 국을 끓여
대령하였더니
우짼 일이냐며
눈이 휘둥그레지는 아내
처음으로
시인 남편 만나기를 잘했다며
감동을 한다

The Scene in the Woods: 965

On my wife's birthday,
I pinned the morning star on her left chest
That I picked from the sky last night
And cooked for her with my poor cooking skills.
Rice cooked with the fragrance of wild rose,
Her favorite scent,
A bowl of Jian egg soup,
A plate of fried dewdrops,
Strawberries
Picked from the moon,
And soup cooked with
Barrenwort from the underworld
Were served at the table.
Did you make all these?
Her eyes widened.
Deeply moved,
For the first time,
She told me she is lucky to have a poet husband.

산골풍경: 977

천년
저 버드나무
곡선 좀 보아요

곡선은 물결치고
볼륨은 흔들리고
리듬은 찰랑이고

여자를 만들 때
저 버드나무를 보고
만들었나 봐요

아내의 곡선과
버드나무의 곡선
아내의 볼륨과
버드나무의 볼륨
아내의 리듬과
버드나무의 리듬
우째 그리 똑 같은고

The Scene in the Woods: 977

A thousand-year-old
Willow tree!
Look at her figure,

Waving curves,
Swinging bosoms,
And swishing rhythm.

When god made women,
He must have made them
In the form of willow trees.

Wife's curve is like
That of the willow,
Her bosom is like
That of the willow.
And her rhythm is like
That of the willow.
How much they are alike!

산골풍경: 979

남자들은
아내의 감동을 저금하며 산다
그래서
남자들이 모이면
서로 자기 아내를 자랑하고
다시 태어나도
지금의 아내와 살고 싶어 한다

여자들은
남편의 거슬림을 저금하며 산다
그래서
여자들이 모이면
서로 남편 흉을 보고
다시 태어나도
다른 남자와 살고 싶어 한다

남자들은 왜
감동을 저금하면서 살고
여자들은 왜
거슬림을 저금하며 사는가
그것은 나도 모르지요

The Scene in the Woods: 979

We men
Deposit virtues of our wives in the heart.
So,
When we get together,
We boast of our wives,
Wanting to live with them,
Even in our next lives.

They women,
Deposit faults of their husbands in the heart.
So,
When they get together,
They speak ill of their husbands,
Wanting to live with other men,
Even in their next lives.

Why do men
Deposit virtues,
And why do women
Deposit faults?
Who would know?

산골풍경: 988

나라님
나라님
나라님 곳간에는
무엇으로 가득한가요

대감님
대감님
대감님 곳간에는 또
무엇으로 가득한가요

우리집 곳간을 보여 줄까요
새 소리 한 가마니
바람소리 한 가마니
밤 안개 한 가마니
꽃 구름 한 가마니
이런 것들로 가득합니다

The Scene in the Woods: 988

Your Majesty,
Your Majesty,
What is in your treasury?
What is it filled with?

Your Excellency,
Your Excellency,
What is in your treasury?
What is it filled with?

Do you want to see my treasury?
A bag of bird calls,
A bag of sighing wind,
A bag of night fog,
And a bag of glowing clouds.
Mine is filled with these.

산골풍경: 993

연분홍 살내음이
문틈으로 스미길래
가만 문을 열고
바라보는 산골

밤안개 하얀 이불을 펴놓고
열 아홉 살 반달 아가씨가
목욕을 하고 있습니다

나도 몰래 포르르 날아간 나는
나도 몰래 반달을 품은
범인이 되고 말았습니다

내일에 내가 보이지 않거든
달나라 영창에 갔을 거라고
그렇게 그렇게만 말해 주세요

The Scene in the Woods: 993

The fragrance of pale pink skin
Leaking through the crevice
Made me open the door
And gaze at the woods.

A nineteen-year-old Lady Half-moon
Spread the white night fog bedding
And took a bath.

I secretly flew up to the moon
And made love to the Lady Half-moon.
I became the most wanted fugitive.

If you can't find me tomorrow,
I will be in jail on the moon.
Please tell her so.

산골풍경: 999

구멍 숭숭 뚫린
허물어질 것 같은
우리집 곳간이지만
이 곳간에는
무릉도원이 있고
극락이 있고
천국이 있습니다
천국에서 살고 싶으면
곳간 빗장을 풀고
새소리 한 가마니 안고 와
가만히 풀어 놓으면
우리 집은 온통 천국이 되고
극락에서 살고 싶으면
오로라 한 가마니 안고 와
가만히 풀어 놓으면
우리집은 온통 극락이 되고
무릉도원에서 살고 싶으면
꽃송이 한 가마니 안고 와
가만히 풀어 놓으면

우리집은 온통 무릉도원이 됩니다
이렇듯
구멍 숭숭 뚫린 우리 집 초가 곳간에는
천국과 극락과 무릉도원이
가득 쌓여있습니다

The Scene in the Woods: 999

In my many-holed,
On the verge of falling apart
Treasury of mine,
There are
The Peach Blossom Spring[7],
Sukhavati[8],
and heaven.
If I want to live in heaven,
I open my treasury,
Take out a bag of bird calls
And spread it
To make my house heaven.
If I want to live in Sukhavati,
I take out a bag of the aurora
And spread it
To make my house a Sukhavati.
If I want to live in the Peach Blossom Spring,
I take out a bag of flowers
And spread it

To make my house the Peach Blossom Spring.
Like so,
In my many-holed straw-roofed treasury in the house,
Heaven, Sukhavati, and the Peach Blossom Spring
Are piled up in full.

7) The Peach Blossom Spring: An ethereal utopia where the people lead an ideal existence in harmony with nature, unaware of the outside world for centuries that appear in Tao Yuanming's fable. (The Peach Blossom Spring, Wikipedia, 2021)
8) Sukhavati: A pure land in Buddhism commonly known as the Western Paradise. (Sukhavati, Wikipedia, 2021)

산골풍경: 1,025

말로는 다 못해
편지로 해야지
편지 한 장 쓰는데
수수십 년 걸렸나 봐
편지 한 장 손에 들고
그대 찾아 헤메이다가
못 찾고 돌아오며
하늘가에 묻어둔 편지
그 하늘이 어딘가요
내 가슴입니다

The Scene in the Woods: 1,025

Words cannot say,
But a letter could do.
Writing a letter
Took so many decades.
With a single-page letter in my hand,
I have searched for you.
But came back fruitless,
To bury the letter on the edge of a sky.
Where is the sky?
It is in my heart.

산골풍경: 1,037

한 송이
두 송이
날아간 그리움
추억의 산골에
야생화로 피어 있고
하얀꿈
파란꿈
키워 온 영혼
허공으로 날아가
거품으로 떠 있고
한 번
두 번
넘어진 내 인생
가랑잎으로 또르르 말려
겨울나무 가지 끝에
매달려 있습니다

The Scene in the Woods: 1,037

As a flower
And two,
My dissipated longing
Has blossomed into wildflowers
In the woods of my childhood memories.
My soul nourished with
White dreams
And blue dreams
Flew into the air
To float like bubbles.
My life broken
Once
Or twice
Is rolled in withered leaves
And is hung
At the branch tip of a winter tree.

산골풍경: 1,041

서랍 속에 넣어 둔
하얀 그리움을
봄비 내린 다음날에
심었습니다
쑥쑥 자란 나무에
튼실하게 익은 열매
따먹어야지 나무를 흔든다
저런저런
떨어지지 않고
열매가 새가 되어 날아가네요
그리움의 나무엔
과일이 아니라
새가 열렸어요

The Scene in the Woods: 1,041

I planted in my yard
A white yearning
Kept in the drawer
On the day after a spring rain.
I shook its trunk
To pick the luscious fruit
From the mature tree
Oh well,
Fruits did not fall
But turned into birds and flew away.
My tree of yearning
Do not bear fruits
But birds.

산골풍경: 1,047

수만 개의 불혓바닥을
널름거리며
이글거리는 저 하늘에 태양
그 속을 들어가 보셨나요
그 속에는
만년설산이 있습니다
사람들은 태양을 보며
뜨거운 불덩어리만 보인다 하지만
나는 그 속에
차가운 만년설산만 보입니다

The Scene in the Woods: 1,047

The sun
Sprawls millions of fiery tongues
Blazes in the sky.
Have you ever been inside?
Inside,
There is a glacier mountain.
Many look upon the sun
And see the burning core.
But I
Only see a sharp glacier mountain.

산골풍경: 1,048

소나무 위에
구름을 펴 놓고
구름 위에 돗자리를 깔고
신선과
번개가 마주 앉아
바둑을 두고 있다
산그늘이 내리는데
오늘도 끝나지 않았는가
어제 두던 바둑을
오늘도 두고 있다

The Scene in the Woods: 1,048

On a pine tree,
Spread a sheet of cloud,
Laid a carpet on the cloud,
And sitting face to face,
A hermit and a thunder
Play the game of Go.
A mountain shadow is casting down.
Is not the game over yet?
The game of Go from yesterday
Is still on.

산골풍경: 1,054

꽃은
걱정을 모르고
웃으며 살고 있고

냇물은
장애물을 모르고
노래하며 살고 있고
나무는 운명을 모르고
춤을 추며 살고 있다

나도 세살 적엔
저랬는데
지식에 오염되고부터
걱정 속에서 살고 있고
욕심을 알고부터
노래 없이 살고 있고
운명을 만나고부터
춤을 잃고 살고 있다

The Scene in the Woods: 1,054

Flowers
That know no worries
Smile as long as they live.
Streams of water
That know no obstacles
Sing as long as they live.
Trees that know no fate
Dance as long as they live.
When I was three years old,
I lived like them.
Knowledge infected me
To live in worry,
Knowing greed
Put an end to my melody,
And encountering fate
Made me forget how to dance.